The Norfin® Trolls

Laugh Out Loud

A Book of Jokes and Riddles

by Beth Goodman

Illustrated by Cathy Beylon

SCHOLASTIC INC.

New York Toronto London Auckland Sydney

ISBN 0-590-45925-2

Copyright © 1992 by The Troll Company, Aps.
All rights reserved. Published by Scholastic Inc.,
730 Broadway, New York, NY 10003, by arrangement with
EFS Marketing Associates, Inc.
NORFIN is a registered trademark of EFS Marketing Associates, Inc.

12 11 10 9 8 7 6 5 4 3 2 1   2 3 4 5 6 7/9

Printed in the U.S.A.   24

First Scholastic printing, September 1992

You Deserve a Laugh Today!

Why did the Norfin Troll tell jokes to the mirror?

He wanted to see it crack up!

You'll find lots of other rib-tickling,
giggle-grabbing riddles in this book.
So laugh along with the Norfin Trolls!

What did the Wizard of Norf get when he crossed a clown and a chicken?

A comedi-hen!

What did the Wizard of Norf get when he crossed a banana peel with a banana peel?

A pair of slippers!

Rookie Norfin's Home Run Ha Ha's!

Why did the troll team sign a two-headed baseball player?

To play the doubleheaders!

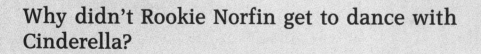

Why didn't Rookie Norfin get to dance with Cinderella?

Because he missed the ball!

What has 18 legs, red spots, and catches flies?

A baseball team with measles!

What's the worst weather for trolls and mice?

When it's raining *cats* and dogs!

Why couldn't Noah play cards on the ark?

A giant troll was standing on the deck!

Why did Officer McNorfin hope the rain would keep up?

So it wouldn't come down!

How do you make a troll float?

Two scoops of ice cream, soda water, and one troll!

Trolling Along the Beach!

Why did the Norfin Playmates cross the ocean?

To get to the other tide!

What did the beach say when the tide finally came in?

Long time, no sea!

Do sharks like to act in movies?

Only if they get big, juicy parts!

What game do cousins Inge and Sven play at the seashore?

Troll-ey ball!

Why do troll bakers always want dough?

They knead it!

Why is Chef Norfini mean?

Because he beats the eggs, whips the cream, and mashes the potatoes!

Fairy Tales from the Wizard of Norf!

Why did the Sleeping Beauty Norfin sleep for one hundred years?

Her alarm clock was broken!

Which fairy tale is about a girl who was ordered to clean house for one hundred years?

Sweeping Beauty!

What's a pig's favorite fairy tale?

Slopping Beauty!

Where is the best place to see a troll-eating fish?

At a seafood restaurant!

What do you call a troll carpenter who misplaces his tools?

A saw loser!

Clowning around with Norfin Jesters!

What happened to the troll cannonball at the circus?

He got fired!

Why do ponies make poor ringmasters?

Because you can't shout if you're a little horse!

Where do troll acrobats learn to walk the tight rope?

High school!

Why do trained seals always know what's happening?

They're always on the ball!

What kind of fruit do trolls feed scarecrows?

Strawberries!

Imagine you were Norfin Witch Wanda trapped in a spooky house full of ghosts. What would you do?

Stop imagining!

The Joke Troll of Fame!

How can you tell Rock 'N Troll from spaghetti?

Rock 'N Troll doesn't slip off the end of your fork!

Rock 'N Troll: Is it hard to spot a leopard?
Neandertroll: No, they come that way!

Norfahontas: How do you make a snake cry?
Inge: Take away its rattle!

When a baby Norfin cries at night, who gets up?

The whole neighborhood!

What did Grandma Norfin do when she found a dinosaur in her tub?

She pulled the plug and washed it down the drain.

Down on the Farm with Farmer Troll

Why did the troll farmer's cow yawn when she got up in the morning?

It was just an udder day!

What insect does well in school?

A spelling bee!

How do rabbits travel?

By hareplane!

What is a frog's favorite game?

Hop scotch!

What do you call the troll football championship game?

The Troll Bowl!

How does Astronorf greet a two-headed martian?

Hello! Hello!

Why did the troll cross the road?

To get to the other side!